FORGIVENESS

THE SUPERHIGHWAY TO BLISS

by

Julia Robinson

Forgiveness: The Superhighway to Bliss

ISBN: 9781706933502

Independently published

To Daumants Willow of Many Things.

May you be only Peace, Love and Happiness.

We could begin with the premise that every loving thought is true, everything else is an appeal for healing and help, regardless of the form it takes. Only appreciation is an appropriate response to another. Gratitude is due them for both their loving thoughts and their appeals for help, for both are capable of bringing love into your awareness if you perceive them truly. All your sense of strain comes from your attempts not to do just this.

From 'A Course in Miracles'
(pronouns neutralised).

Forgiveness is a powerful way to live. When we have an unexamined experience, we pack it into a corner of the subconscious where deep down in the dark it grows into a belief. Strange right? Our tightly held beliefs are not assessed! As I've gone deeper and deeper into the making of this book, or rather as the book has gone deeper and deeper into the unmaking of me, like a magnet, it has pulled tangled beliefs out of my mind for me to let go of them. This is called forgiveness. It's sometimes an easy process and sometimes a really thorn-scratchy tumble where in the midst of it all I wonder if I am actually, properly, for real, going insane. The truth is the exact opposite.

'Out with the darkness; in with the light!' I shout in celebration down the corridors of being. It is the most rewarding state I have ever felt. To be simply being, opening petal-like to Joy, Peace and Happiness. Forgiveness is a sweet awakening out from the dream of projection into the extension of Love.

It is so simple, and so easy to overlook.

Once in a drama therapy workshop with Jungian psychologists we were told that when caged animals are set free, on seeing the door swing open, they often stay put, right there – they do not budge. They sit in front of the open door. Freedom is not their comfort zone any longer. Their comfort zone is being captive.

These animals are not the only ones in mental cages. When I was working in an orphanage in Nepal for women and girls there was a woman living nearby in a small, squalid bathroom with her four children. Toni, the heart behind the project, offered her a place in the orphanage: her own room for her and her children. There would be washing facilities too, other women to support her, regular food and her children could go to school. But there was no way to get that lady out of her bathroom. She knew the space. She knew how to handle herself and her children within those confines, she knew the ins and outs of that tiny, little bathroom...she did not know anything else. Better the devil you know that the devil you don't. She stayed in the bathroom.

And in this predicament, we also find ourselves.

There are many ways to forgive and set ourselves free, this book describes one of them. When things get trickier and I can't clear my mind, I use other techniques that I'd like to share as additional tools. There is an excellent worksheet within the book by Colin Tipping called *Radical Forgiveness: Making Room for the Miracle* which he also gives as a free tool on his website radicalforgiveness.com. I have used this worksheet over and over and every time, without exception, it has been a deeply nourishing and cleansing experience. It prompts me to see how I have been catching myself (again) within a prison of my own making and that all I need do is allow my belief system be turned around, or even better, dissolved.

There's another tool that I've only just started to use. It is a facebook app called *Spiri* developed by a team from *A Course in Miracles*. It is a robot: it is predictable. It gathers in my emotional information. I kind of like it not being human and instead a totally and utterly non-judging bot without the capacity to care a damn about me or my answers. No one is peering in to glimpse my most embarrassing pants-down-no-toilet-paper state of being. I can dig deep in that privacy and tell the bot my darkest secrets.

Then logically, uncaringly, it reconfigures the order of these frightening, vulnerable revelations as data! And with an emoji it offers a different order of perception. The reversed 'thinking' is totally revealing – so much so I realise the person inflicting the pain is me and the one I need to forgive is, indeed, myself.

In my opinion, forgiving oneself is a far more difficult process, but it would appear all healing comes from forgiving ourselves – for distancing ourselves from the light of Peace, Joy and Happiness; and we do this by believing in voluminous clouds of obscure beliefs that are simply NOT TRUE.

Being able to let go of dogged-eared, well-loved beliefs, at first seems absolutely bonkers. (WTF? I can see it with my own eyes…! What is it exactly that you didn't get? Do you want me to tell you the story again?) Trusting the process more and more, I summon up the tremendous strength to open to the idea that *maybe* what I believe is simply dead wrong. I mutter, begrudgingly, 'OK, just for the next 5 minutes, I'm going to try – only for sake of the experience – to think about this another way'.

As a result, miracles have occurred.

Instead of being a rejected fool I realise I have been given the gift of freedom! Instead of being scapegoated I realise I have been healed and can allow others to heal with me. Instead of being attacked I realise I have been asked to open to love. It is so powerful. It is so heart-warming. It is so, Me. The real Me. The 'I am' when the Ego is not.

There is a beautiful Argentinian phrase, 'Dios es donde vos no sos' (God is where you are not). Take away the Ego and we are naturally Eternally Divine. God is Love and without the Ego that's what we are too.

Divinity

We don't know
how to be
and yet we are.

Which leads us nicely into forgiveness as the Superhighway into Love – and becoming It. I wish this miracle for all of humanity, for in truth we are all One.

love Julia xxx

THIS IS A TRUE STORY

(ANY PHYSICAL LIKENESS IS UNINTENTIONAL)

I say something
(hoping for a certain response)
BLANKET OF APPROVAL
nice, warm feelings
I washed the dishes

no response?

The gap is really between our idealised self and the self we feel we are being.

MIND THE GAP !!
NICE WARM FEELINGS
Is he thinking my worse fears?
no response???
NAGGING FEARS OF WHO MAYBE I AM

If we cannot accept ourselves as we are ...

We project ourselves everywhere
DO NOT LOOK INSIDE
WARNING

FAMDANMILY

Projection separates us

from ourselves

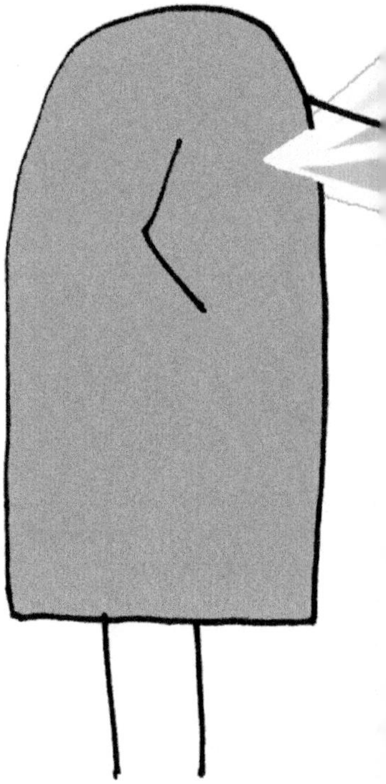

PROJECTIONS ABOUT HOW IMPORTANT I AM
A LOVELESS TRAGEDY
I will call this 'The Return of the Prodigal Son'.
Real Self

... and from others

Is it true the next-doors' car is better than mine? Is it?
Whoops... what did she say?!!

Crazy goat

Jung said,
Someone brave enough to withdraw their projections is an individual who is conscious of a pretty thick shadow...
FEAR
GUILT
TERROR
ANGER

and...
Such a person knows that whatever is wrong with the world...
... is in themselves

Outside is silent.

Innocent.

meaningless.

Neutral.

Take the philosophical question:

If a tree falls in a forest and no-one hears

- did it make a sound?

scientists have discovered
the answer is:
NO.
It creates waves that our brains interpret as sound. We hear it only inside our minds

We interpret the world

as our

BODY

HORMONES
SYNAPSES, DNA
ORGANS ETC

and

MIND

EXPERIENCES
SELF IMAGE
PROJECTIONS ETC

dictate.

Any stress, non-peace, bad feelings, pain isn't caused for the reasons we believe.

Let's imagine the world as:

a **VIDEO**

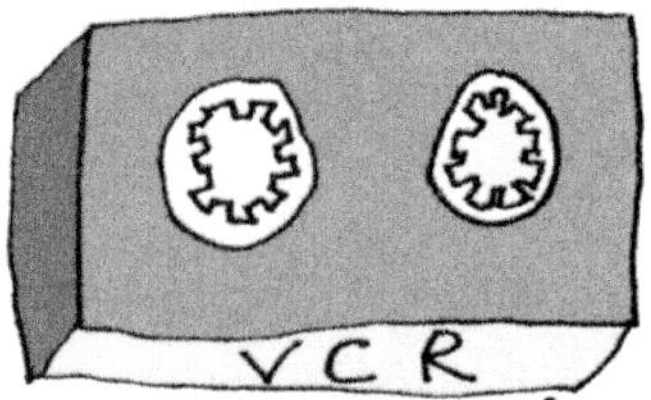

(aka MP4)

with **AUDIO**

plus us with

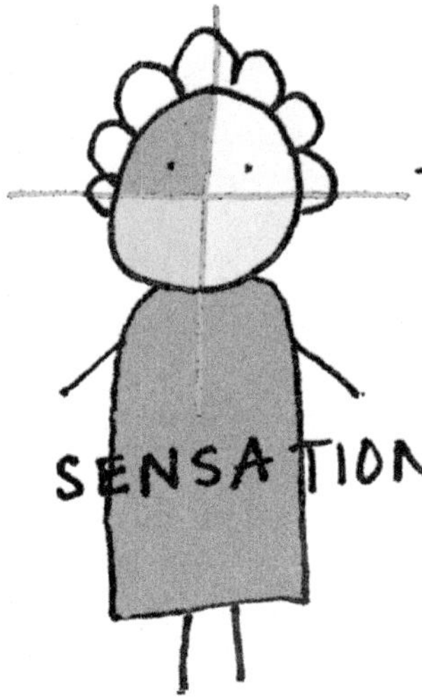

(aka personality)

And beholding ourselves in time we further perceive our own projections with the added ingredients of

What we perceive through the body senses (body eyes, body ears etc) is
INNOCENT
This tree falling is neither positive or negative: it is just a picture.
BUT...

EGO

adds a little trick:

it conjures up perception.

which, obviously, is a cause of suffering.

The pain in the mind is then also perceived in the body image & makes us believe

This **PAIN** and **MISERY** is **REAL**

And, in pure madness,
we choose separation
due to fear rather
than

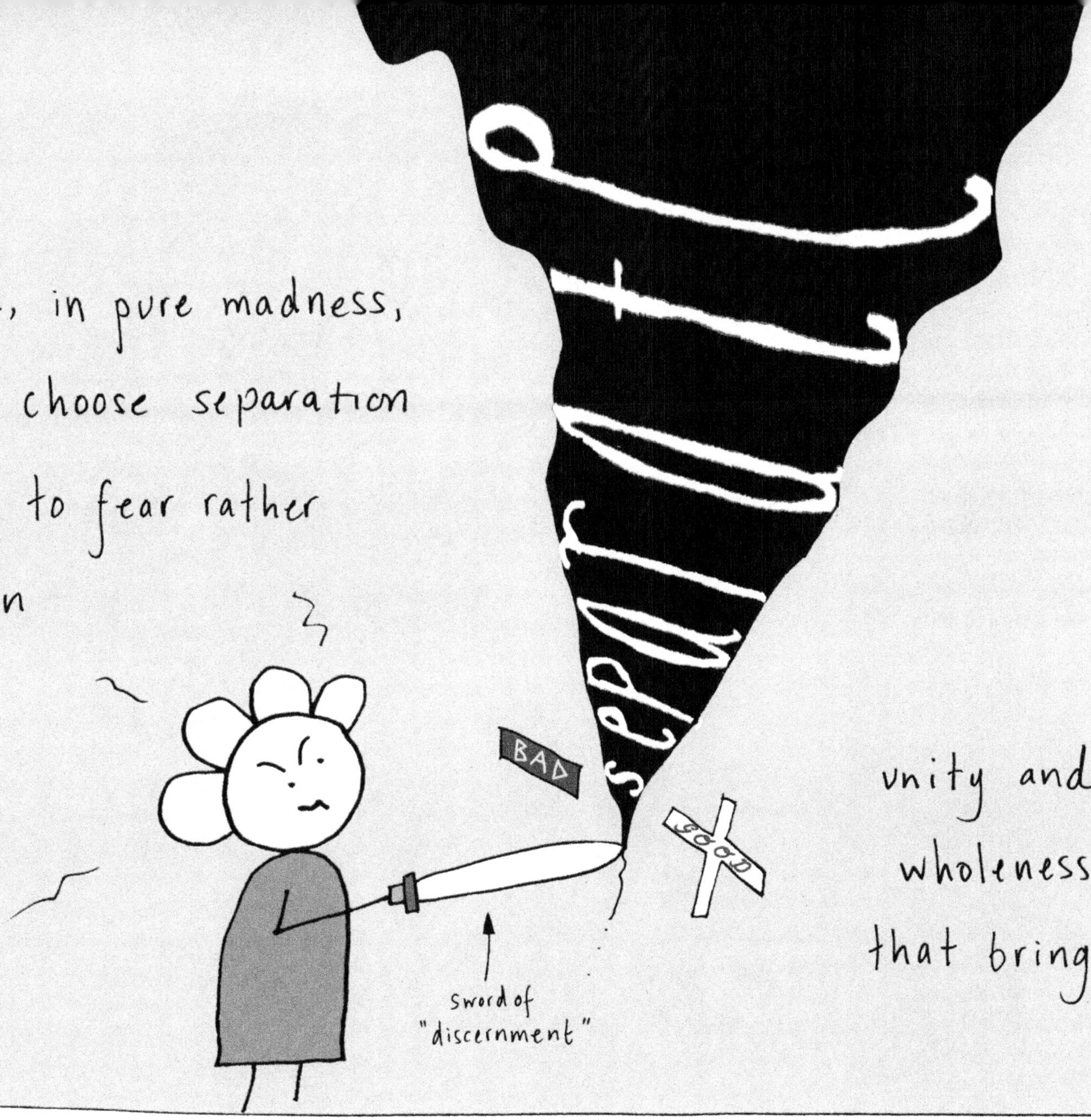

unity and
wholeness
that bring

love, peace, happiness...

THE EGO is everything
you 'see' that isn't real.

Sages throughout eternity have taught:
if we are at One with All
we recall our <u>true</u> Selves.

Forgiving others is really forgiving ourselves for having chosen not to be happy.

When you make the feelings (and perceptions) disappear - what you see

FAMILY

So **how** to FORGIVE ?

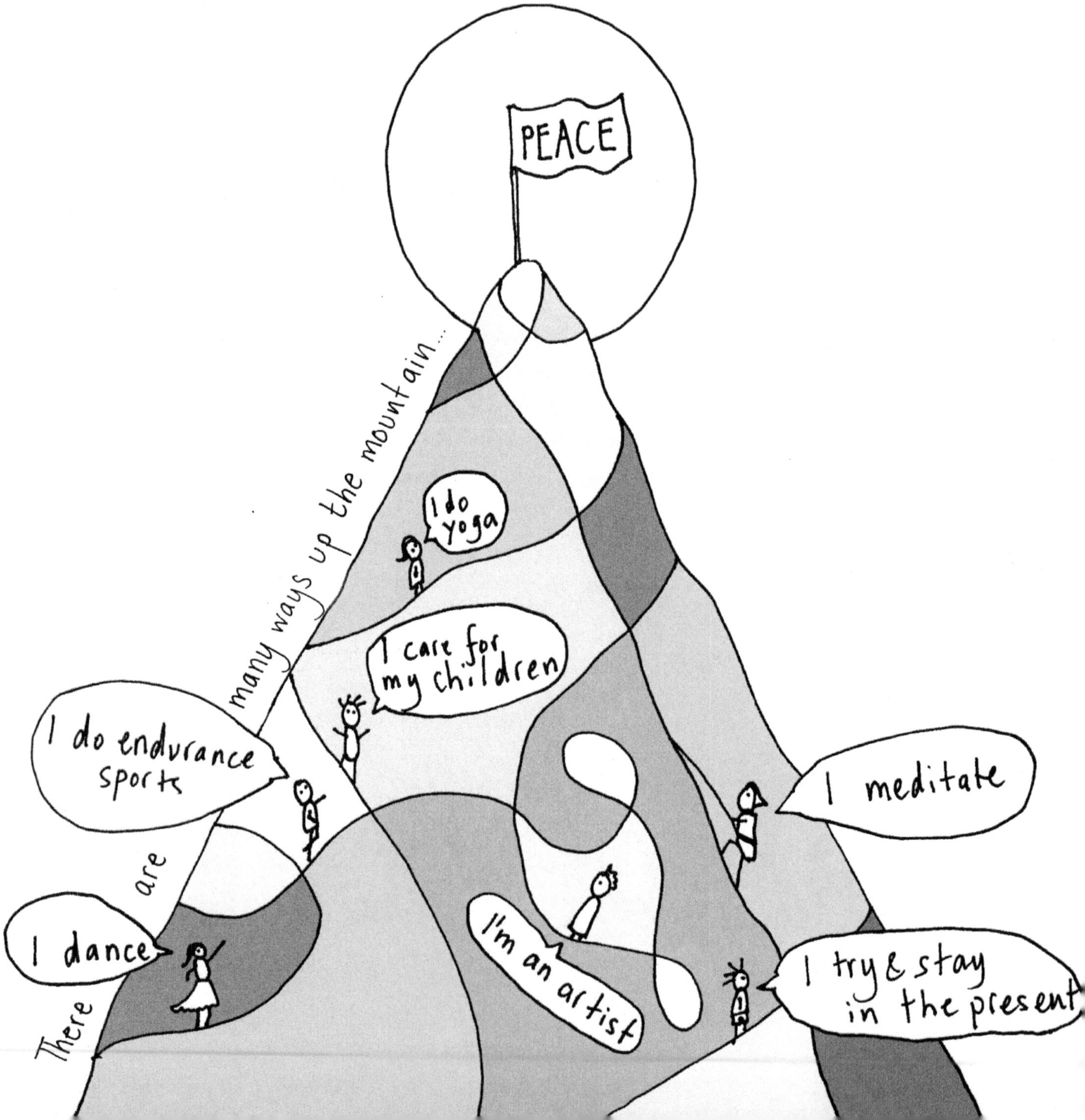
PEACE
There are many ways up the mountain....
I do yoga
I care for my children
I do endurance sports
I meditate
I dance
I'm an artist
I try & stay in the present

The Truth lies in
the Simple but it is
where most overlook.

This is my way:

I force my mind
to go into blank,
to empty,
to stop rolling
in the unpleasant.

crazy goat

This isn't happening anymore... why hold on?
crazy goat

Ahhh!

Forgetting inner clouds is synonymous with forgiving.

It feels
DIVINE

I realise I had been self harming.

Ridiculous

- really!

None of this is happening <u>now</u>!

... if ever.

Often there's a struggle
(which is yet another Ego trick)

It also needs **discipline** of the **MIND**

to become feather soft

and in hard moments **faith**
that you can do it

Training the monkey mind takes patience: out of ten experiences of ego projection maybe you'll notice & remember to forgive **ONCE**, and it gives strength in the next ten to forgive **TWICE** and in the next ten **3 TIMES...**

ETC ETC ETC ETC

and again...

Suddenly our peace is shattered
I am right!
I am right!
by an ego-treasured moment...

IN CASE OF
EMERGENCY
START
AGAIN
BREAK BUBBLE

The future isn't now

The past isn't now

We forget to remember

In Holy Moments we are able to drop anger, shame, entitlement etc...

The Red Sea parting!

Other times the Ego appears more real

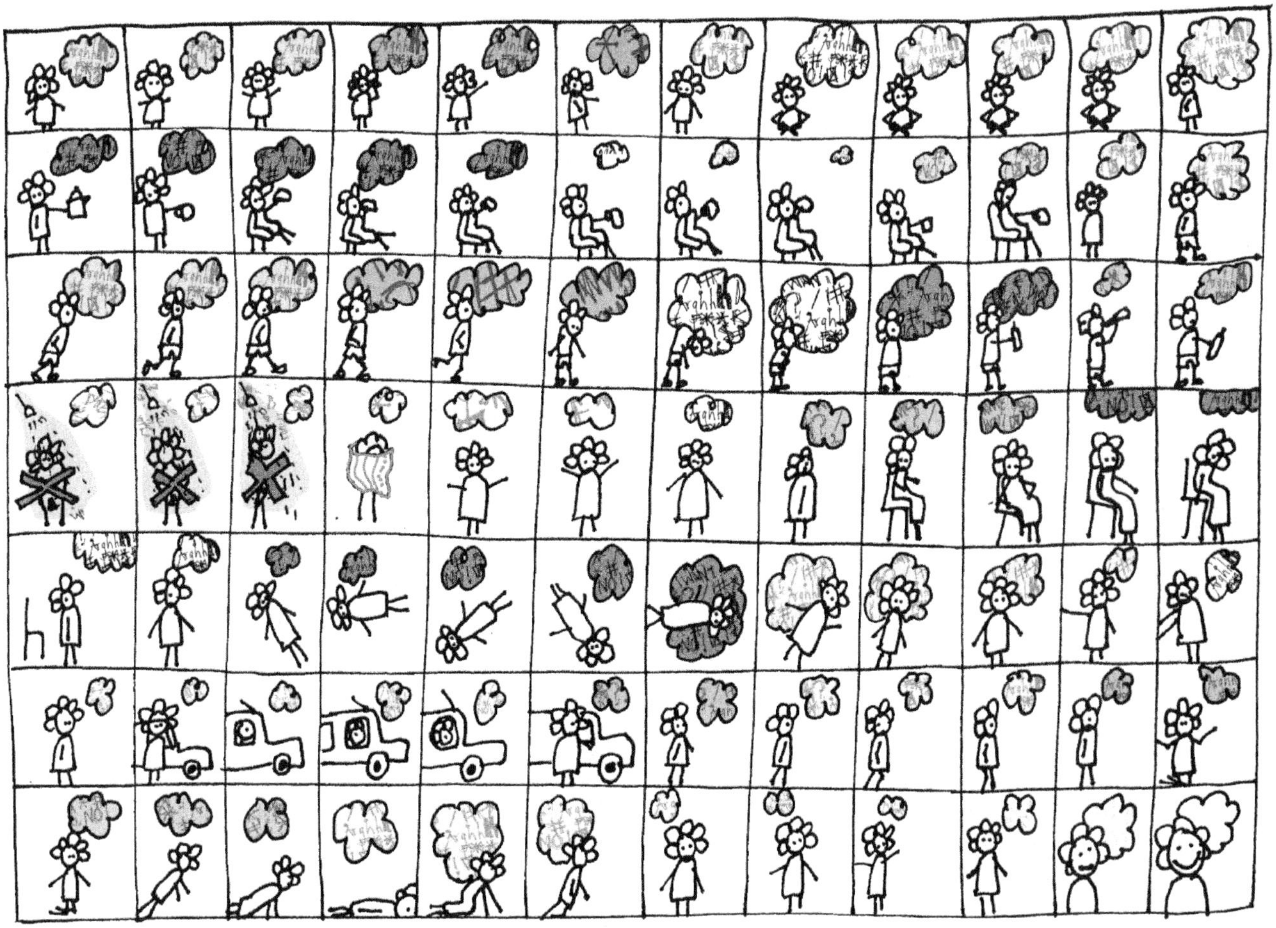

STING!

Forgiving others is really forgiving the clouds in us that separate us from our

TRUE SELVES

from
MYSELF
to
self

Which do want to see (in yourself and in others)?

Anger
Fear
Guilt

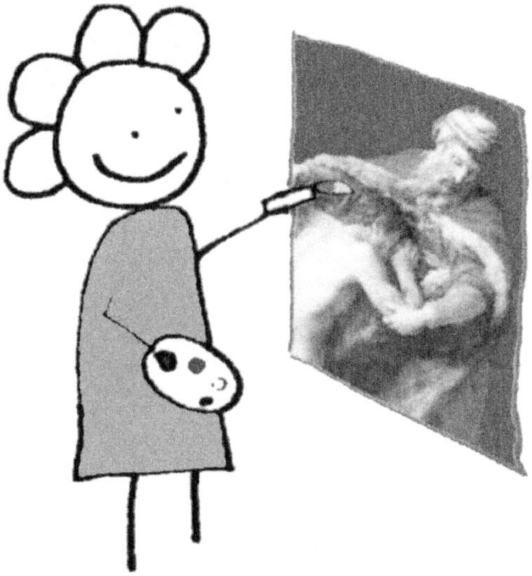

Peace
Flow ♡
Happiness

Ego Excludes

Love Expands

The more we forgive, the more we can be in the present, with our hearts open.

And from that place of expansion, sharing our True Selves, we can create without limits.

In those **Holy Moments**

we create space for

MIRACLES to occur.

And we clear space
to live in greater

PEACE

Joy and

Happiness.

Life becomes so **FULL OF EASE.**

WARNING: CAN TURN INTO A PUMPKIN. WHEN FIRST RIDING USE VIGILANCE AND RELAXED CONCENTRATION

It feels so, so

Free

Joy
Peace
happiness

It feels wonderful...

YOU TOO ARE (LIKE) THE WORLD:

INNOCENT

(really!)

The real you

AND SO YOU CAN FORGIVE *yourself* TOO

And the messy emotions you have just on your own...

Guilt
Anger
Fear
PAIN
WHY?
Fears
Fears
Don't see me
FEARS
bla
bla
bla
b
blab
NOBODY LOVES ME
DISLIKE
LIKE
Why is no-one seeing me
Guilt
victim
victim
victim
See me
WHO?
*!#
*!#
FEARS

This too is forgiving ourselves for having chosen not to be happy.

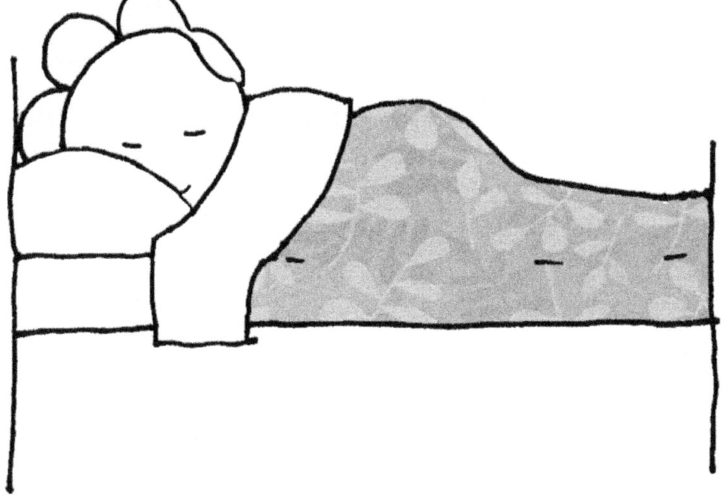

It is <u>that</u> simple;

& that hard.

In this state I see with my heart

everything is as it is:

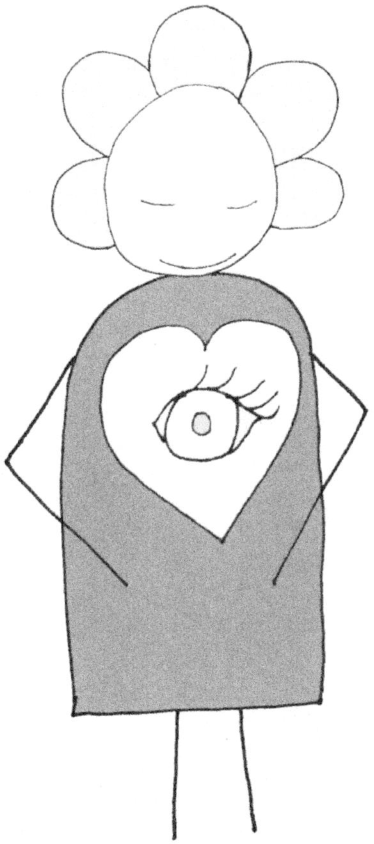

Nothing needs
to be done
Nothing needs
to be fixed

to be in

Peace, Joy and Happiness.

TO LOVE
AND BE LOVED
IS CHILD'S PLAY

Forgiving allows

us to become

EVER MORE
PEACEFUL

Projection or forgiveness?

It really is your choice.

(And maybe your <u>only</u> choice).

Menu

GROUND HOG DAY

1. Project

OR

2. Expand

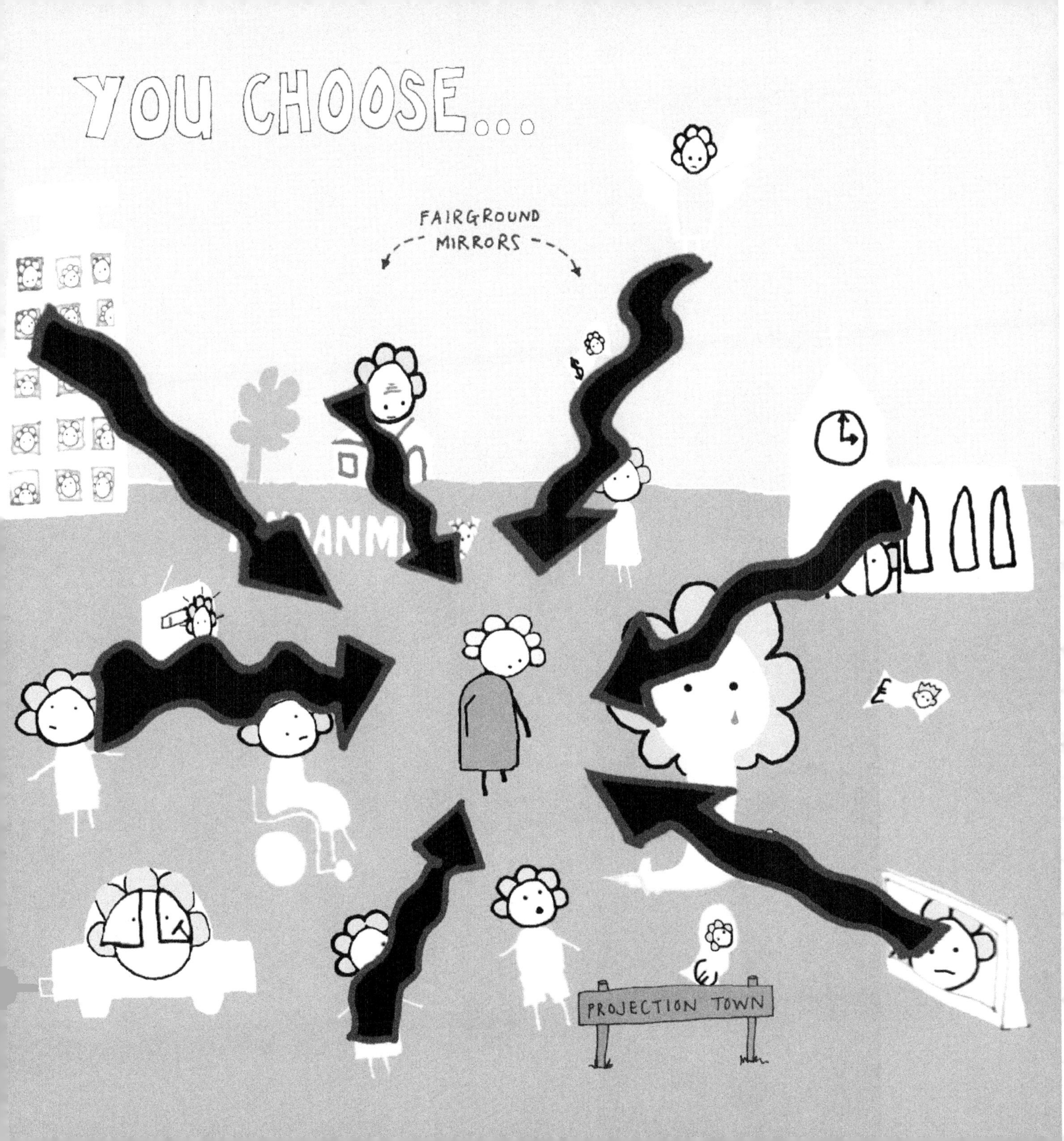
YOU CHOOSE...
FAIRGROUND MIRRORS
PROJECTION TOWN

...OR

May you find
Yourself

Within

GRACE

POST SCRIPT:

I am so happy with this book, so content, so proud, but there is a niggling doubt at the back of my mind that the way I describe making the mind go blank is only good for me. We each have our own path into healing.

So, consider this book a blueprint of a journey, not to be emulated, copied or praised (though my ego whispers, 'Praise me, pretty please!') See it as a signpost to be either followed or turned away from on your own journey into further Peace, Joy and Happiness.

What I *can* say though, with surety, is that forgiveness is a universal gateway to the place where forgiveness is not needed anymore. *The Course of Miracles* is guiding me on the beautiful path of forgiveness to allow me to connect more with what is real. This book is based on these experiences.

Forgiveness is the superhighway to Love's presence.
May you find your limousine.

Julia Robinson has spent her life out of the box, hitchhiking around the world, floating down the Amazon in a self-made raft, selling roasted chickens in Argentina, working at an orphanage in Nepal, studying a masters in Jungian psychology in Catalonia, going to art school in Greece, dancing and writing in the States and living in nature in England. She is presently loving making music and writing in Latvia.

She has a curious mind, an adventurous spirit and ants in her pants. She travels much more now to the realms within, guided by *The Course in Miracles* from where the ideas in this graphic existential essay have been inspired.

For more word whirlation, poems and information please visit:

www.intenselypersonal.com

love Julia xxx

BEDTIME STORIES FOR ADULTS

Thanks for reading!!

More books by Julia Robinson

Bedtime Stories for Adults

Poetry

Poetry

Prose

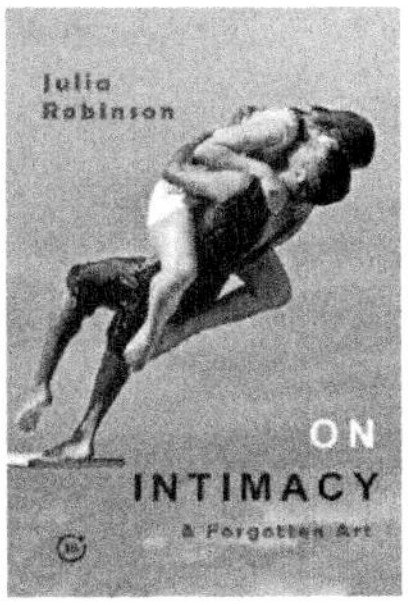

For more information please visit www.intenselypersonal.com
or search for any of these books/ebooks on Amazon

Printed in Great Britain
by Amazon

79387204R00066